Fun Fan Facts:
The Unofficial NBA Edition

Toronto Raptors

Everything Young Raptors Fans Should Know

By: Jake Liam

Dedication

For every fan who ever stood outside in the cold, watched on a screen they couldn't quite see, and cheered anyway. We The North means all of you.

THE NBA
BY THE NUMBERS

MOST NBA CHAMPIONSHIPS*

CELTICS (18)
LAKERS (17)
WARRIORS (7)
BULLS (6)
SPURS (5)

As of the 2024-25 Season. † One Trophy = 4 Championships.

NBA HISTORY SNAPSHOT

1946 NBA Founded

1954 Shot Clock Introduced

1979 3-Point Line Added

2023 NBA Cup Introduced

BIG NUMBERS

$156 million
Stephen Curry's est. earnings in the 24-25 season

7'7"
Tallest player in NBA history (Gheorghe Mureşan & Manute Bol)

30 | 4 | 82

Teams Competing in the NBA

Playoff Rounds

Games Per Season

TORONTO RAPTORS
IN THE NBA

- FOUNDED: 1995†
- NBA TITLES: 1
- CONFERENCE TITLES: 1*

1
Title That Shocked the World

*† Founding dates are complicated & may cause arguments at Thanksgiving. Ask someone born before color TV. All Titles reflect pre-relocation franchise history. * As of 2024-25 Season.*

NBA ALL-TIME MVP LEADERS

KAREEM ABDUL-JABBAR (6) ★ MICHAEL JORDAN (5) ★ BILL RUSSELL (5)

EASTERN CONFERENCE

Atlantic – **Celtics**
Atlantic – **Nets**
Atlantic – **Knicks**
Atlantic – **76ers**
Atlantic – **Raptors**
Central – **Bulls**
Central – **Cavaliers**
Central – **Pistons**
Central – **Pacers**
Central – **Bucks**
Southeast – **Hawks**
Southeast – **Hornets**
Southeast – **Heat**
Southeast – **Magic**
Southeast – **Wizards**

WESTERN CONFERENCE

Pacific – **Lakers**
Pacific – **Clippers**
Pacific – **Warriors**
Pacific – **Suns**
Pacific – **Kings**
Northwest – **Nuggets**
Northwest – **Timberwolves**
Northwest – **Thunder**
Northwest – **Trail Blazers**
Northwest – **Jazz**
Southwest – **Mavericks**
Southwest – **Rockets**
Southwest – **Spurs**
Southwest – **Pelicans**
Southwest – **Grizzlies**

Introduction

Welcome, fans! Whether you're new to cheering for the Toronto Raptors or you've been bleeding the team colors your whole life, this book is packed with fun, exciting facts about your favorite team. Get ready to impress your friends and family with everything you know about the Raptors.

Quick Time Out

This book is packed with stats. Like, A LOT of stats. Every fact was checked, double-checked, and triple-checked. But here's the thing about basketball history: not everyone agrees on everything. Ask someone who watched games before color TV and someone who grew up with instant replay and you'll get two completely different answers. My dad, stepdad, uncle, and grandpa all argued about the same fact. Four people. Four answers. All of them think they're right. So if you spot something that doesn't match what you've heard, congratulations. You might be a bigger fan than the people who helped make this book. And honestly? That's pretty cool.

HOW IT WORKS

THE SEASON
82 Games. One Goal.
Each team plays 82 games.
Win enough to make the
Playoffs.
Every game counts!

PLAYOFFS
30 Teams. 16 Make It.
8 per conference make the playoffs.
Win=Advance | Lose=Go Home
Best record
gets home court!

PLAYOFF ROUNDS
Best of 7. Win 4 or Go Home.
4 rounds of pure pressure.
Every series is do-or-die!

OVERTIME?
5 More Minutes.
Keep playing until
someone pulls ahead.
No ties. Ever.

THE FINALS
One Series. One Champion.
Winner lifts the Trophy.
Legend status unlocked.

How the NBA Works

At first glance, basketball feels simple. Ten players. One ball. Two hoops. Go.

Then the NBA adds the layers.

An 82-game regular season. A draft where bad teams pick first. Playoffs that last two full months. Superstars who can change everything with one trade. Dynasties that rise, fall, and rise again.

And somehow, it all works.

The NBA is built on one big idea: every team gets a chance to reset, reload, and rise again. No relegation. No dropping down to a lower league. Just basketball, every night, from October through June.

It is a league designed for drama, stars, and comebacks. And once you understand the flow, it is impossible to stop watching.

The League Setup

The NBA has 30 teams, spread across the United States and Canada. Those teams are split into two conferences:

- Eastern Conference
- Western Conference

Each conference has three divisions, mostly based on geography. Divisions matter for scheduling, but not as much as they used to.

Every team plays 82 regular season games, usually from October through April. Home games. Road games. Back-to-back nights. Long road trips. The season is a marathon before the sprint even starts.

Win games, and you climb the standings. Lose too many, and the pressure builds fast.

How Games Are Played

An NBA game has four quarters, each lasting 12 minutes. That means 48 minutes of game time, plus timeouts, free throws, and the occasional coach argument that adds another 20 minutes nobody planned for.

Scoring is simple:

- A shot inside the three-point line is worth 2 points
- A shot beyond the arc is worth 3 points
- Free throws are worth 1 point

If the score is tied at the end of regulation, the game goes to overtime, which lasts 5 minutes. Still tied? Another overtime. Keep going until someone wins.

There is a shot clock too. Teams have 24 seconds to take a shot. No standing around. No holding the ball forever. Keep it moving.

The Regular Season Race

The regular season is long for a reason. It tests everything.

Depth. Health. Focus. Patience.

Teams play opponents from both conferences, but they face conference rivals more often. By the end of the season, each conference's top teams have earned their playoff spots the hard way.

The goal is simple: make the playoffs. But there is a twist.

The NBA Cup

In 2023, the NBA added something new to the middle of the season. Something with actual stakes. They called it the In-Season Tournament, now known as the NBA Cup.

It works like this: Every team plays a small group stage during November and December, with special court designs that look like nothing else in basketball. The best teams advance to a knockout round held in Las Vegas.

The winners split a prize pool. Players earn bonus money. And for the first time, a team could lift a trophy before the playoffs even started.

Some fans are still warming up to it. Some players love it. But the moment a team starts treating it seriously and a crowd shows up buzzing in December, it feels like something.

Which, honestly, sounds about right.

The Play-In Tournament

Instead of sending the top eight teams from each conference straight to the playoffs, the NBA added something new. The Play-In Tournament.

Here is how it works:

- Teams ranked 1 through 6 in each conference are safe
- Teams ranked 7 through 10 fight for the final two playoff spots

The 7 and 8 seeds have an advantage. Win once and you are in. Lose and you still get one more shot. The 9 and 10 seeds have to win twice in a row just to earn a first-round matchup.

It turns the end of the season into a sprint. Every game suddenly matters more. Fans love it. Coaches age rapidly.

The NBA Playoffs

Once the playoffs begin, everything tightens.

Sixteen teams enter. Eight from each conference. Every round is a best-of-seven games series. That means the first team to win four games moves on:

- First Round
- Conference Semifinals
- Conference Finals
- NBA Finals

Home-court advantage matters. Crowds get louder. Rotations get shorter. Superstars play heavier minutes. One bad quarter can flip a series. One great performance can define a career.

By the time the NBA Finals arrive in June, only two teams are left. One from the East. One from the West.

Four wins away from a championship. Four wins away from history.

The NBA Draft: Hope Begins Here

Here is where the NBA gets clever. Every summer, new players enter the league through the NBA Draft. Teams take turns selecting college players, international stars, and teenagers straight out of high school.

The teams that finished with the worst records get the best odds to pick early through the Draft Lottery. It is not guaranteed, but it gives struggling franchises a real shot at changing their future with one pick.

That means one bad season does not doom you forever. It might actually change everything. Some franchises are rebuilt by a single draft night moment.

Hope shows up wearing a new jersey.

No Relegation. All Pressure.

Unlike many global sports leagues, NBA teams never drop down to a lower league. They always stay in the NBA.

That does not mean there is no pressure.

Fans remember losing seasons. Owners make changes. Coaches get replaced. Players get traded. Every year is a test of direction, patience, and belief.

Stars, Systems, and Showtime

The NBA is famous for its stars. But stars do not win alone.

Teams need chemistry. Coaches need systems. Role players need to deliver on the biggest stages. One injury. One hot streak. One trade deadline deal. Any of it can flip a season.

That balance between individual brilliance and team basketball is what makes the league special.

Fast breaks. Buzzer-beaters. Game 7s. And moments that get replayed forever. That is the NBA.

Once you get the flow, it is pure electricity.

Toronto Raptors Facts

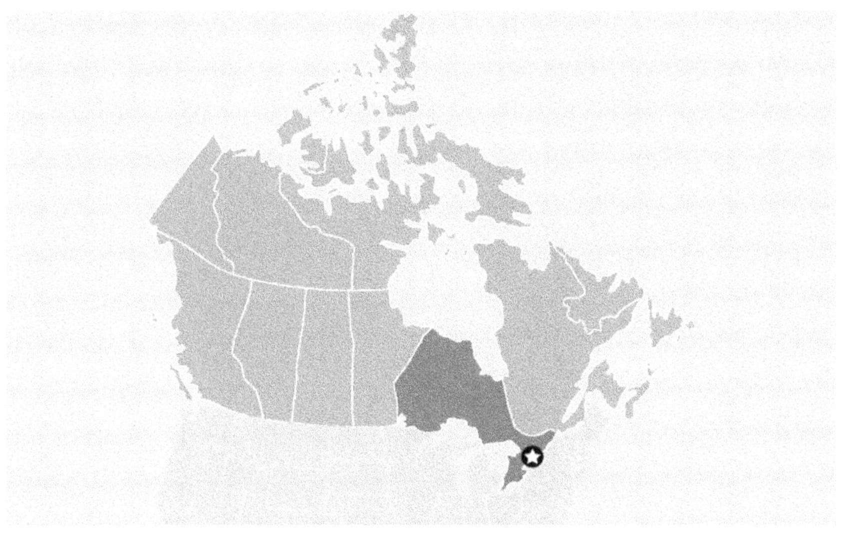

Home City

Toronto, Ontario, Canada

Home City Metro Area Population

about 6.4 million

Home Arena

Scotiabank Arena

Max Capacity: 19,800

Famous Local Food

Butter tarts, poutine, peameal bacon sandwiches, Tim Hortons

Conference / Division

Eastern / Atlantic

Chapter 1: The North Rises

1. A Name Born From a Movie

In 1993, a little film called Jurassic Park landed in theatres and completely broke people's brains. Kids everywhere were obsessed with one dinosaur in particular: the Velociraptor. Fast, terrifying, and absolutely not something you wanted chasing you through a kitchen.

When the NBA awarded Toronto its expansion franchise in 1994, the team held a public naming contest. Thousands of entries came flooding in. People suggested the Towers. The Hogs. Someone, somewhere, submitted the Tarantulas with full confidence. The Raptors won in a landslide, riding a wave of dinosaur fever that only 1994 could produce.

The original logo featured a purple dinosaur palming a basketball. With tiny T-rex arms. Which, if you stop and think about it for even three seconds, is a physical impossibility that nobody questioned for years. Welcome to the NBA, Toronto.

2. One Country, One Team

When the NBA announced it was expanding into Canada, two cities got franchises marking the first time NBA basketball had been played on Canadian soil professionally. The Vancouver Grizzlies and the Toronto Raptors both tipped off in the 1995-96 season.

For Toronto, this was enormous. Canada had produced hockey legends, Olympic sprinters, and more than its share of comedians. But a major pro basketball team? That was new. The Raptors immediately became something bigger than a franchise. They became a symbol that basketball belonged everywhere, not just in the United States.

Vancouver did not make it. The Grizzlies packed up and relocated to Memphis in 2001, leaving Toronto as the only Canadian team in the league. The entire country adopted the Raptors. That is a lot of pressure for one purple dinosaur mascot to carry. More on that mascot later.

3. The Rough Early Years (and Why They Had to Happen)

Here is a fun way to think about the Raptors' first few seasons: imagine building a house by starting with just the foundation and a sandwich. That was basically Toronto in 1995.

The team's first real star was point guard Damon Stoudamire, who won the NBA's Rookie of the Year award in 1996 and gave Toronto fans something to cheer about. He was listed at five feet ten inches, which made him one of the shortest players in the league, and somehow one of the most exciting to watch. He made believers out of a brand-new fanbase.

But the wins were hard to come by. The early Raptors lost a lot of games. They finished 21-61 in that first season, which is not a typo. Building something from scratch takes time, and Toronto was building from absolute zero. Those rough years mattered, though. Every losing season planted seeds. The fans who stuck around through the bad times made the good times, eventually, feel like something no other city could understand.

4. From SkyDome to Scotiabank, and the Meaning of The Six

The Raptors played their first two seasons inside SkyDome, a baseball and football stadium better known for having a hotel inside it with rooms overlooking the field. It worked. Barely. But it worked.

In 1999, the team moved into their permanent home, a purpose-built arena then called the Air Canada Centre. It was renamed Scotiabank Arena in 2018 after a corporate sponsorship deal. The building holds around 19,800 fans for basketball, sits right in the heart of downtown Toronto, and over time became one of the loudest arenas in the league on a big night.

As for "The Six," the nickname for Toronto has a few possible origin stories. The most popular version credits Drake, who started using it around 2014 and made it famous in his music. It is generally thought to refer to the six boroughs that merged in 1998. Though some connect it to the old 416 area code. Drake has never given a single clean explanation, which is on-brand for someone who made a whole career out of keeping people guessing.

5. We The North

Before 2014, the Raptors were a team without an identity. Good enough to watch, not good enough to fear, and not yet famous for anything except Vince Carter highlights that were already a decade old.

Then the marketing agency Sid Lee came up with three words: We The North. The campaign launched ahead of the 2014-15 season and hit like a truck. The idea was simple but sharp. Every other team in the NBA was American. Toronto was not. They were from somewhere else, somewhere colder, somewhere that had been waiting a long time to be taken seriously. We The North said all of that without saying any of it.

The slogan spread from ads to arenas to tattoos faster than most people expected. By the time the 2019 championship run arrived, those three words had been spray-painted on spirit boards, lit up on buildings, and shouted by thousands of fans packed into Jurassic Park outside the arena. Not bad for a tagline. Not bad at all.

6. The Man Who Put Toronto on the Basketball Map: Vince Carter "Air Canada" (1998-2004)

Vince Carter arrived in Toronto via a draft-night trade in 1998, and within about eighteen months, he had made himself one of the most exciting players on the entire planet. That is not an exaggeration. That is just what happened.

He won the 2000 Slam Dunk Contest with a performance that people still argue about. He threw down a 360-degree windmill. He dangled his entire forearm through the rim on one dunk. He did a between-the-legs slam so clean it looked computer-generated. The judges gave him perfect 50s. Fans started calling him Air Canada, a nod to both his home country and his seemingly unlimited ability to stay suspended in the air longer than any human reasonably should.

At the 2000 Sydney Olympics, playing for Team USA, Carter leaped completely over seven-foot-two-inch French center Frederic Weis for a dunk that stopped the broadcast for several seconds while the announcers tried to figure out what they had just seen. Carter wore number 15 for the Raptors and sparked what many people call the Vince Carter Effect. He didn't just create fans. He inspired an entire generation of Canadian kids, often referred to as Vince's Kids, to pick up a basketball. By the time he left, he had helped inspire the next generation of NBA superstars, like Shai Gilgeous-Alexander and Jamal Murray, to one day wear the Maple Leaf on their jerseys.

7. The One Who Got Away: Tracy McGrady "T-Mac" (1997-2000)

Here is a detail that surprises people who did not follow basketball in the late 1990s: Vince Carter and Tracy McGrady played on the same team at the same time. They are cousins. And for a brief window, Toronto had both of them.

McGrady was drafted ninth overall in 1997, one year before Carter arrived. He was raw, young, and clearly had something special brewing. He averaged modest numbers in his first few seasons, mostly coming off the bench and learning on the job. Then Carter showed up, the crowd went electric, and Toronto looked like it might have something.

McGrady left as a free agent in 2000, heading to Orlando where he became one of the most gifted scorers in the league. He won back-to-back scoring titles in 2002-03 and 2003-04. Looking back, having two future superstars on one roster that young, in that city, in that era, felt like a kind of lightning that only strikes once. Toronto got to see the spark. They just did not get to keep the bolt.

8. The Quiet Cornerstone: Chris Bosh "CB4" (2003-2010)

If Vince Carter was the player who made Toronto fall in love with basketball, Chris Bosh was the player who kept that relationship alive through the hard times.

Bosh was drafted fourth overall in 2003 out of Georgia Tech, and he spent seven seasons in Toronto giving the franchise something it badly needed: consistency. He was long, skilled, and almost impossible to stop around the basket. He made multiple All-Star appearances as a Raptor and became the franchise leader in several statistical categories during his time there.

He was also doing all of this on a team that was rarely very good, which takes a specific kind of mental toughness that does not always get enough credit. Bosh left for Miami in 2010 to join LeBron James and Dwyane Wade, which stung in Toronto the way any departure of that size stings. He went on to win two championships with the Heat. In 2021, he was inducted into the Naismith Basketball Hall of Fame. Toronto fans who watched him grind through those middle years always knew he belonged there.

9. The Heart of Everything: Kyle Lowry "KLow" (2012-2021)

Kyle Lowry was not always considered a franchise cornerstone. When he arrived in Toronto via trade from Houston in 2012, he was seen as a solid backup option and maybe a decent starter. He turned that evaluation into one of the more spectacular pieces of underselling in NBA history.

Lowry became the engine of the most successful era in Raptors history. He was listed at six feet tall, which made him shorter than most NBA guards, and he played like someone who had heard that fact and found it deeply funny. He was physical, fearless, and the kind of point guard who genuinely seemed to enjoy the messiest moments of the biggest games.

He made multiple All-Star teams as a Raptor and was on the floor for every important Raptors moment from 2012 through 2019. The championship. The late-game stops. The possessions where Toronto needed someone to refuse to lose. Lowry was usually in the middle of all of it. He left for Miami in 2021 after nine seasons, and the tribute video Toronto played for him on his return visit was long and deserved.

10. The Kid from Compton Who Became a Toronto Legend: DeMar DeRozan (2009-2018)

DeMar DeRozan grew up in Compton, California, one of the toughest neighborhoods in Los Angeles. He was drafted ninth overall by Toronto in 2009, and over nine seasons he became one of the most beloved players in franchise history. Which is a remarkable outcome for someone who came to a Canadian city at age nineteen having never really left Southern California.

DeRozan was a scorer in the old-school mold: mid-range jumpers, trips to the free throw line, relentless drives to the basket. He made multiple All-Star teams as a Raptor and quietly put together one of the best careers in franchise history. He and Kyle

Lowry became one of the most dependable backcourt pairings in the East.

In the summer of 2018, the Raptors traded DeRozan to San Antonio in exchange for Kawhi Leonard. DeRozan found out the way most people find out bad news they never saw coming: suddenly, and not at all gently. He had publicly said he trusted Toronto with his future, which made the trade hit harder than most. He handled it with class, went on to star with the Spurs and later Chicago, and remains one of the more beloved figures in Raptors history despite never being part of what came next. Sometimes the story works out best for everyone except the person at the centre of it.

11. One Ring, One Year, One City

The 2019 NBA Finals should not have gone the way they did. At least, that is what most people outside Toronto thought going in.

The Golden State Warriors had just won two straight championships and three of the previous four. They had Stephen Curry, Klay Thompson, and Draymond Green. They were the machine everyone else measured themselves against. Toronto had a roster of good players, a brilliant coach in Nick Nurse, and one rental superstar who had spent the whole season playing behind a wall of mystery. The Raptors were supposed to make it interesting. They were not supposed to win.

They won in six games. Kawhi Leonard was named Finals MVP. Fred VanVleet, who had gone undrafted out of college and signed with Toronto as a free agent nobody was fighting over, hit shot after enormous shot. The city of Toronto produced one of the loudest collective reactions any sporting event has ever generated in Canada. The parade drew an estimated two million people onto the streets. For context, that is roughly the population of Houston showing up to one giant block party.

12. The Four Bounces That Broke Philadelphia

Game 7. Second round. 2019 playoffs. Toronto versus Philadelphia. 92-90 Philadelphia with 4.2 seconds left.

Kyle Lowry pushed the ball up the court and found Kawhi Leonard near the right corner. Leonard caught it, turned, and launched a high-arcing shot over the outstretched hand of Joel Embiid just as the buzzer sounded. The ball hit the rim. Then it hit the rim again. Then again. Then one more time. Four bounces, each one making roughly forty thousand people in the building hold their breath in a way that should probably require medical supervision. Then, it fell in.

The shot is now simply called The Shot, which tells you everything about how it landed in Toronto's memory. One of the only buzzer-beaters in NBA history to end a Game 7, it sent the Raptors to the Eastern Conference Finals and sent Philadelphia into an offseason of extremely complicated feelings. Four bounces. Four. If even one goes differently, the whole 2019 championship story looks completely different. Luck

and greatness arrived at the same time, which is usually
how the best sports moments work.

Kawhi Leonard rarely celebrates early. He just lets the game do the talking. In the 2019 playoffs, he delivered a Game 7 buzzer-beater that bounced four times on the rim before dropping in. Toronto fans are still reliving every bounce. *Photo: Kawhi Leonard during Game 2 of the 2019 NBA Finals. Source: Wikimedia Commons.*

13. The Complicated Love Story Between Vince Carter and Toronto

The dunk over Frederic Weis at the 2000 Sydney Olympics did not just go viral. It bounced back to Toronto. Every time that clip circulated, every time someone watched Carter clear a seven-foot-two French center like he was stepping over a speed bump, the first thing people associated with it was not Team USA. It was the Toronto Raptors. That is what Carter did for this franchise. He made Toronto the home address of the most jaw-dropping basketball on the planet.

Which is what made the ending so painful. By 2004, with the team struggling and his relationship with the organization breaking down publicly, Carter requested a trade. The Raptors sent him to New Jersey in December of that year. The reaction from Toronto fans was volcanic. For years afterward he was booed so loudly on return visits that the building shook for the wrong reasons.

Here is where the story finds its real ending. Over time the anger faded and the highlights took over again. The generation of Canadian kids he had inspired grew up and started giving him the credit he deserved. When Carter retired in 2020 after 22 seasons, Toronto honored him properly. He called his relationship with the Raptors the most important of his career. The city believed him. Not every love story is clean. This one just needed twenty years to make sense.

14. The Trade That Changed Everything

In the summer of 2018, the Raptors made a move that their own fanbase largely did not want them to make.

They traded DeMar DeRozan, their longtime star and a player who had publicly expressed trust in the organization, to San Antonio in exchange for Kawhi Leonard. Leonard had played only nine games the previous season due to a quad injury, had reportedly clashed with the Spurs organization, and had made clear he was not planning to re-sign with whoever traded for him. Toronto was essentially betting its entire franchise on a one-year rental.

Kawhi was healthy, dominant, and exactly what Toronto needed. He played 60 regular season games, led the Raptors through a historic playoff run, and delivered the championship. Then he signed with the LA Clippers in free agency and flew to Los Angeles, because that had always been the plan. General manager Masai Ujiri made the kind of trade that could have ended his career or defined it. It defined it. Not every gamble deserves to win. This one did.

15. Scottie Barnes and the Reason to Stay Interested

After Kawhi left, a lot of people assumed Toronto would enter a quiet few years. They were not entirely wrong, but they were not entirely right either.

In the 2021 draft, the Raptors selected Scottie Barnes with the fourth overall pick. Barnes was not the consensus top prospect coming in, and Toronto's choice raised a few eyebrows from people who had expected them to go a different direction. Barnes promptly won the NBA Rookie of the Year award. He was creative with the ball, versatile on defense, and seemed to genuinely enjoy the chaos of close games rather than retreating from it.

Barnes developed into one of the more interesting young players in the Eastern Conference, the kind of player who fills up a box score in ways that do not always make the highlight reel but consistently make the coaching staff happy. The post-championship rebuild was always going to take patience. Barnes is the reason that patience has felt worth it.

16. Drake, Official Anything

Most teams have celebrities who show up courtside and wave at cameras. Toronto gave Drake a job title.

In 2013, the Raptors made Drake their official Global Ambassador, which is a real thing that happened and that is listed in real press materials. His responsibilities included being very famous near the team, appearing in promotional content, and showing up to games in outfits that generated their own news cycle. He delivered on all three.

Drake grew up in Toronto and has spent most of his career making sure everyone knows exactly where he is from. The Raptors partnership was genuine in the way that most celebrity sports arrangements are not. He redesigned the team's warm-up uniforms. He wore a coaching staff vest during the 2019 championship run. He sometimes stood close enough to the opposing bench during games that the NBA had to send a memo about it. Giving a globally famous recording artist an official role with your basketball team is either genius branding or an ongoing experiment with no control group. Possibly both.

17. The Raptor, a Mascot With No Fear and No Apologies

The Raptors' mascot is simply called The Raptor, and he has been a fixture of the franchise since the beginning, with one notable interruption.

In the early years, the team actually used two mascots: The Raptor and a secondary dinosaur called Stripes. Stripes did not survive the rebranding era of the early 2000s. The Raptor did, and over time became one of the more entertaining mascot performers in the league, known for elaborate on-court gags, interactions with players that push the limits of what professional athletes will tolerate, and a general energy that could charitably be described as unregulated.

Mascot performers are rarely named publicly during their tenure, so the identities of the people inside the costume over the years are not always verifiable. What is consistently verifiable is the reaction The Raptor gets at Scotiabank Arena, which is loud, warm, and occasionally involves small children having mixed feelings about how close he gets during timeouts.

18. Nav Bhatia, the Superfan Who Became a Legend

Nav Bhatia immigrated to Canada from India in 1984. He built a successful career as a car dealer in Toronto, and in 1995, the year the Raptors played their first game, he bought season tickets. He has not missed a home game since.

Bhatia became one of the most recognizable faces in the building, always in his section, always loud, always in Raptors gear. The team eventually gave him the official title of Superfan, which was not a promotional stunt but more of an acknowledgment that he had been there before almost anyone else and had stayed through everything. He has been recognized at the arena during games, brought family and friends by the hundreds over the years, and become something of an ambassador for what it means to adopt a team completely.

In 2021, the Naismith Basketball Hall of Fame inducted Nav Bhatia as part of its Contributor category. He is believed to be the first fan ever inducted into a professional basketball hall of fame, though the Hall of Fame designation categories have evolved over the years. Either way, it is the kind of story that is almost too feel-good to be real, and it is completely real.

19. Jurassic Park, the Outdoor Cathedral

During big playoff runs, Maple Leaf Square, the plaza outside Scotiabank Arena, transforms into something the Raptors and their fans call Jurassic Park. Giant screens go up. Food trucks appear. Thousands of people who could not get tickets inside fill the streets and watch every possession like they have a personal stake in the outcome.

During the 2019 championship run, the crowds at Jurassic Park became part of the story themselves. Television broadcasts regularly cut to the outdoor crowd during timeouts. The noise from outside reportedly traveled into the arena on some nights. At one point, city officials estimated more than fifteen thousand people were packed into the plaza for a single game, which is roughly the capacity of several NBA arenas.

Jurassic Park is not unique to Toronto in concept but feels unique to Toronto in execution. The intensity of a crowd that chose to stand outside in Canadian spring weather, sometimes in the rain, for three hours because they needed to be near the thing they cared about, is its own kind of sports fact.

20. One Country, No Limits

The Raptors are the NBA's only team based in Canada, often seen as representing the country's basketball identity.

Over the years, Canada has become a genuine basketball pipeline. Players like Andrew Wiggins, Shai Gilgeous-Alexander, Jamal Murray, and RJ Barrett all grew up in Canada during the era when the Raptors normalized the idea that Canadian kids could play at the highest level. Whether all of those players became Raptors is beside the point. The Raptors made basketball feel like a national sport in a country that had one national sport and was not expecting company.

The team regularly draws fans from cities across Canada who fly to Toronto for home games. The fanbase extends into provinces that do not have a local team of any kind. Representing Canada is not a marketing line for the Raptors. It is a structural reality that shapes how the franchise thinks about itself and its place in the league.

Chapter 5: The North Isn't Done

21. The Man Who Built It, and What He Left Behind

Every championship team has a player who gets the trophy and a person nobody outside the building fully understands who made the whole thing possible. For the Toronto Raptors, that person was Masai Ujiri.

As of the mid-2020s, Ujiri remained one of the key figures who shaped the Raptors organization after more than a decade of leadership. Born in Nigeria, he had worked his way up from unpaid scout to NBA Executive of the Year before arriving in Toronto with a philosophy built on boldness and a willingness to make moves that looked wrong before they looked right. The DeRozan-for-Kawhi trade is the most famous example. He also founded Giants of Africa, a nonprofit that builds basketball courts and runs camps across the continent, giving kids access to the game in communities that had never had it.

In 2025, Ujiri and the Raptors parted ways after thirteen seasons, leaving behind one championship banner and a franchise that knew what it felt like to be the best team in the world. Bobby Webster, who had been GM under Ujiri since 2017, took the reins. The organization Ujiri built did not disappear when he walked out the door. It just became someone else's job to carry it forward.

22. Building Without a Blueprint

Most NBA rebuilds follow a recognizable pattern. Lose games, collect draft picks, land a high lottery pick, hope he turns into something. The Raptors have never been especially comfortable with that approach.

After the Kawhi departure in 2019, Toronto chose to stay competitive rather than bottom out. They kept veterans, developed young players, and tried to maintain an identity even when the roster was in genuine transition. The results were mixed in terms of wins and losses, but the organization consistently resisted the idea that suffering through years of bad basketball was the only path back.

That philosophy involves real risk. Draft position matters in the NBA, and teams that try to stay in the middle of the standings often end up with neither a great young player nor a championship-caliber roster. Whether Toronto's approach pays off is a question still being answered. But the refusal to simply wave a white flag and wait says something about how the franchise sees itself.

23. The 905: Where Raptors Are Made

Not every NBA player arrives with a first-round draft pick attached to their name and a highlight reel that broke the internet. Some of them start somewhere quieter, in front of smaller crowds, proving themselves one game at a time until someone upstairs takes notice.

The Raptors 905 are Toronto's G League affiliate, named after the area code that surrounds the city of Toronto. They play in Mississauga, Ontario, just outside the city limits, and over the years have become one of the more respected player development pipelines in the league. The G League is essentially the NBA's minor league system, where players on the edge of rosters get real game experience instead of sitting at the end of a bench hoping their number gets called.

The most famous product of that system in Raptors history is Fred VanVleet, who went completely undrafted out of Wichita State in 2016, signed with Toronto as a free agent, spent time developing with the 905, and eventually became one of the most important players on the 2019 championship team. He went from nobody's draft pick to a guy whose name gets chanted at Scotiabank Arena. The 905 did not make Fred VanVleet, but it gave him the floor space to make himself.

24. One Building, Two Religions

Scotiabank Arena sits in the middle of downtown Toronto and on any given night hosts one of two teams that inspire the kind of loyalty that makes grown adults paint their faces on a Tuesday. The Raptors play there. So do the Toronto Maple Leafs, one of the most storied franchises in NHL history and a team whose fans have been waiting for a Stanley Cup since 1967, which, depending on how you count, is a very long time. But that's a whole other book.

Sharing a building with hockey royalty creates a dynamic that is genuinely unique in North American sports. The Leafs are the default religion in Toronto. They have been for decades. The Raptors arrived in 1995 as the newer, louder, flashier tenant and spent years earning their own place in a city that was not automatically going to hand it over. By 2019, when the championship parade drew two million people into the streets, that argument was pretty much settled.

The two teams are both owned by Maple Leaf Sports and Entertainment, one of the most powerful sports ownership groups in North America. MLSE also owns Toronto FC of Major League Soccer and several other franchises, which means one organization controls an enormous share of the sporting conversation in Canada's largest city.

25. We The North, Still

The Raptors enter the mid-2020s as a team in the middle of its own story, which is exactly where a franchise with genuine ambition tends to live.

The 2019 championship proved the organization can build something that wins at the highest level. The years since have been a reminder that doing it once does not mean the blueprint is permanent. Rosters change. Cap situations shift. Young players develop on their own timelines, and the Eastern Conference does not wait for anyone to get comfortable.

What has not changed is the foundation. Toronto is a legitimate NBA city with three decades of history, one championship banner, and a fanbase that showed during the 2019 run what it looks like when an entire country locks in on one team. The next banner has not been won yet, and the road to it will have turns nobody can fully predict. But the Raptors have earned the right to be taken seriously, and the North has no plans to stop.

Bonus Trivia Quiz!

You think you are a true Raptors fan? Try this bonus quiz!

1. What was the main inspiration behind the Toronto Raptors' name when the team held a public naming contest in 1994?

A) A famous Canadian wildlife conservation program
B) The popularity of the Velociraptor following the release of Jurassic Park
C) A suggestion from the city's first mayor
D) The nickname of the team's original head coach

2. Which Raptors player won the NBA Rookie of the Year award in the team's very first season?

A) Tracy McGrady
B) Chris Bosh
C) Damon Stoudamire
D) Vince Carter

3. What does the slogan "We The North" represent about the Toronto Raptors?

A) Their arena is located in the northern part of downtown Toronto
B) They are the only NBA franchise based outside the United States
C) Their head coach came from northern Canada
D) They have won the most championships of any northern division team

4. Vince Carter's famous dunk over Frederic Weis took place at which event?

A) The 2000 NBA Slam Dunk Contest
B) The 1999 NBA Finals
C) The 2000 Sydney Olympics
D) The 2001 NBA All-Star Game

5. Tracy McGrady and Vince Carter were teammates on the Raptors. What is their family connection?

A) They are brothers
B) They are cousins
C) They are childhood best friends from the same neighborhood
D) They have no personal connection outside basketball

6. Chris Bosh spent seven seasons in Toronto before leaving in 2010. Where did he sign as a free agent?

A) Los Angeles Lakers
B) Chicago Bulls
C) San Antonio Spurs
D) Miami Heat

7. Kyle Lowry arrived in Toronto via trade from which team in 2012?

A) Chicago Bulls
B) Houston Rockets
C) Memphis Grizzlies
D) Oklahoma City Thunder

8. What made the Kawhi Leonard buzzer-beater against Philadelphia in the 2019 playoffs particularly unforgettable?

A) It was a half-court shot
B) It bounced on the rim four times before going in
C) Kawhi made it with his eyes closed
D) It came after he had missed five straight shots

9. In the 2019 NBA Finals, Toronto defeated which team to claim the championship?

A) Cleveland Cavaliers
B) Los Angeles Lakers
C) Golden State Warriors
D) Boston Celtics

10. What official role did Drake hold with the Toronto Raptors?

A) Assistant General Manager
B) Creative Director
C) Global Ambassador
D) Director of Player Development

11. What is the name of the outdoor fan gathering area outside Scotiabank Arena during big playoff games?

A) Dino Square
B) The Six Plaza
C) Jurassic Park
D) North Yard

12. Nav Bhatia earned a historic recognition in 2021. What was it?

A) He was named honorary mayor of Toronto
B) He became the first fan inducted into the Naismith Basketball Hall of Fame
C) He was made a co-owner of the Raptors franchise
D) He received the NBA's first Superfan Championship Ring

13. Which player did Toronto receive in exchange for DeMar DeRozan in the 2018 trade with San Antonio?

A) LaMarcus Aldridge
B) Kawhi Leonard
C) Paul George
D) Jimmy Butler

14. Scottie Barnes was selected fourth overall in which NBA Draft?

A) 2019
B) 2020
C) 2021
D) 2022

15. The Vancouver Grizzlies and Toronto Raptors both joined the NBA in the same season. What happened to the Grizzlies?

A) They moved to Seattle in 1999
B) They folded and their players were redistributed
C) They relocated to Memphis in 2001
D) They merged with the Portland Trail Blazers

Super Fan Secret Challenge

Only a true Raptors fan will know this.

(No Answer Provided)

The Raptors' 2019 championship run featured an undrafted free agent who had gone unselected out of college, signed with Toronto, and delivered some of the biggest shots of the entire Finals. He later signed a major contract extension with the Raptors and became a cornerstone of the post-championship roster. Who is this player, what college did he attend, and in which game of the 2019 Finals did he score a then-career playoff high?

Answer Key

1. B) The popularity of the Velociraptor following the release of Jurassic Park

2. C) Damon Stoudamire

3. B) They are the only NBA franchise based outside the United States

4. C) The 2000 Sydney Olympics

5. B) They are cousins

6. D) Miami Heat

7. B) Houston Rockets

8. B) It bounced on the rim four times before going in

9. C) Golden State Warriors

10. C) Global Ambassador

11. C) Jurassic Park

12. B) He became the first fan inducted into the Naismith Basketball Hall of Fame

13. B) Kawhi Leonard

14. C) 2021

15. C) They relocated to Memphis in 2001

NBA PLAYOFF BRACKET

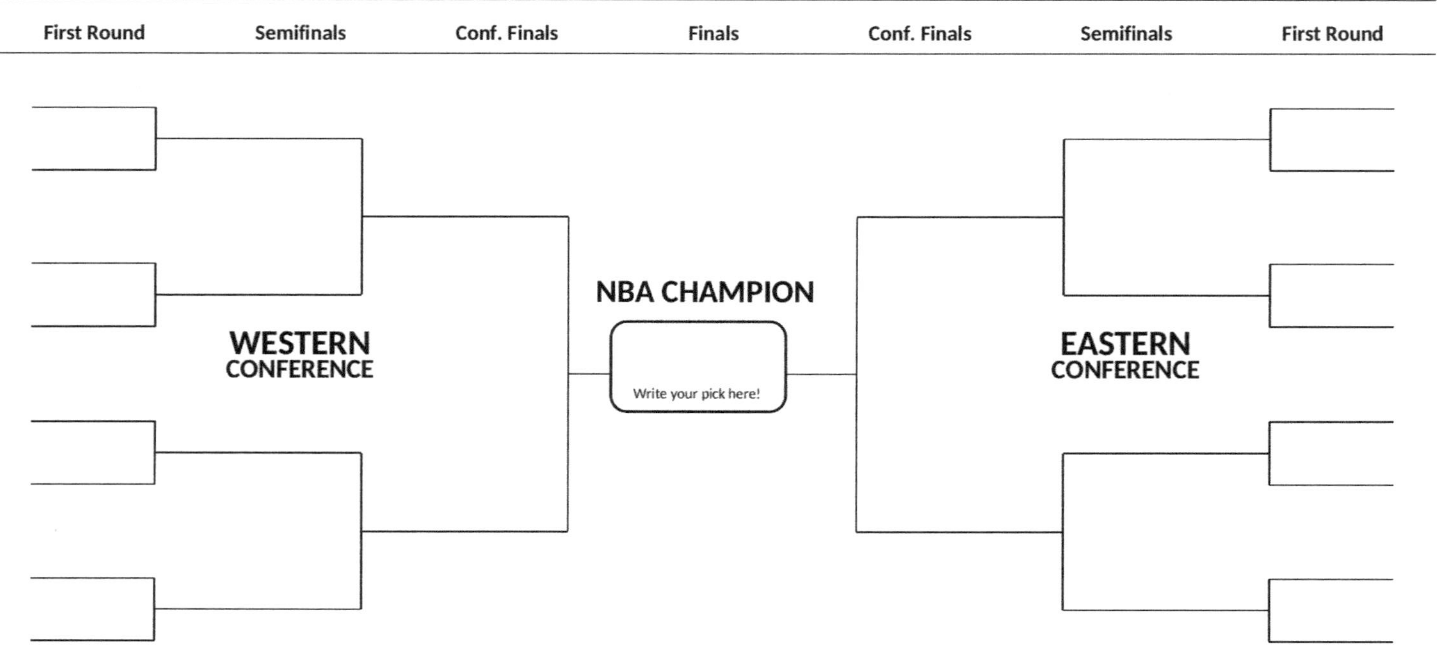

* Fill in your picks and try not to argue with your friends about it!

Part of the Fun Fan Facts: The Unofficial Sports Guide Series

Be the Boss of the Playoffs

You've broken down the matchups. You know which superstar takes over in the fourth quarter. You've seen the bench units that quietly decide series. You've watched the adjustments coaches make when their backs are against the wall.

Now it's time to stop watching and start deciding.

On this page, you are not just a fan. You are the Head Coach drawing up the last play with three seconds left on the clock. You are the GM who built this roster. You are the analyst who saw it all coming.

This is not just filling out a bracket.

This is building your championship run.

Sixteen teams enter the NBA Playoffs. The path is brutal. Best of seven. No shortcuts. No hiding. Every round gets louder, harder, and more personal.

This bracket is your Playoff Control Room.

The Game Plan

1. Survive Round One: Start with the opening round. Which matchup is going seven games? Who has the closer? Who folds under pressure? Make the calls.

2. Feel the Momentum: As you move into the Conference Semifinals and Conference Finals, things change. Role players become heroes. Stars feel the weight. Trust your reads.

3. Own the Finals: Trace your picks all the way to the NBA Finals. When the confetti falls and the trophy is raised, you'll find out who earned it.

House Rules: Circle your boldest upset. That is your official "I knew it" moment.

Choose Your Weapon: Pencil if you want flexibility. Pen if you trust your instincts. Sharpie if you believe in chaos.

Because once the playoffs tip off, there is no rewinding Game 7.

Make your picks. Trust your basketball brain. And let the playoff drama begin.

Fun Facts Wrap-Up

You made it through! You're officially a true superfan! Now it's time to put your knowledge to the test. Share these facts with friends and see who really knows their team best.

Love the series?

Your reviews help other fans discover Fun Fan Facts. If you enjoyed this book, we'd really appreciate you sharing your thoughts and leaving a review.

Want more Fun Fan Facts?

Scan the QR code below to visit our site and explore bonus trivia, challenges, and special extras - including new teams, future series, and collectible fun as they're released.

Collect All the Fun Fan Facts Series!

Check off every book you read. See the full set on Amazon. Search "Fun Fan Facts Jake Liam."

World Cup 2026 Edition

☐ Algeria	☐ France	☐ Paraguay
☐ Argentina	☐ Germany	☐ Portugal
☐ Australia	☐ Ghana	☐ Qatar
☐ Austria	☐ Haiti	☐ Saudi Arabia
☐ Belgium	☐ Iran	☐ Scotland
☐ Brazil	☐ Ivory Coast	☐ Senegal
☐ Canada	☐ Japan	☐ South Africa
☐ Cape Verde	☐ Jordan	☐ South Korea
☐ Colombia	☐ Mexico	☐ Spain
☐ Croatia	☐ Morocco	☐ Switzerland
☐ Curacao	☐ Netherlands	☐ Tunisia
☐ Ecuador	☐ New Zealand	☐ United States
☐ Egypt	☐ Norway	☐ Uruguay
☐ England	☐ Panama	☐ Uzbekistan

World Cup 2026 Group Edition

☐ Group A	☐ Group E	☐ Group I
☐ Group B	☐ Group F	☐ Group J
☐ Group C	☐ Group G	☐ Group K
☐ Group D	☐ Group H	☐ Group L

English Football Edition

☐ Arsenal F.C.

☐ Aston Villa F.C.

☐ Chelsea F.C.

☐ Everton F.C.

☐ Fulham F.C.

☐ Liverpool F.C.

☐ Manchester City

☐ Manchester United

☐ Newcastle United F.C.

☐ Tottenham Hotspur

☐ West Ham United

☐ Wrexham A.F.C.

NBA Edition

☐ Atlanta Hawks

☐ Boston Celtics

☐ Brooklyn Nets

☐ Charlotte Hornets

☐ Chicago Bulls

☐ Cleveland Cavaliers

☐ Dallas Mavericks

☐ Denver Nuggets

☐ Detroit Pistons

☐ Golden State Warriors

☐ Houston Rockets

☐ Indiana Pacers

☐ LA Clippers

☐ Los Angeles Lakers

☐ Memphis Grizzlies

☐ Miami Heat

☐ Milwaukee Bucks

☐ Minnesota Timberwolves

☐ New Orleans Pelicans

☐ New York Knicks

☐ Oklahoma City Thunder

☐ Orlando Magic

☐ Philadelphia 76ers

☐ Phoenix Suns

☐ Portland Trail Blazers

☐ Sacramento Kings

☐ San Antonio Spurs

☐ Toronto Raptors

☐ Utah Jazz

☐ Washington Wizards

About the Author

Jake is a 13-year-old sports fan who loves football, American football, and basketball. He plays soccer as a goalie and dreams of one day playing for West Ham United and helping teach kids to love the game. His passion for sports runs in the family - his dad was a professional baseball player, and his stepdad sparked his love for West Ham. Through the Fun Fan Facts series, he shares the fun and excitement of sports with fans everywhere.